I AM

The Startling Claim of Jesus

JESSE C MIDDENDORF

BEACON HILL PRESS
OF KANSAS CITY

Beacon Hill Press of Kansas City
PO Box 419527
Kansas City, MO 64141
beaconhillbooks.com

978-0-8341-3623-6

Printed in the
United States of America

Cover design: Jeff Gifford
Interior design: Sharon Page

Library of Congress Cataloging-in-Publication Data

Names: Middendorf, Jesse C., author.
Title: I am : the startling claim of Jesus / Jesse C Middendorf.
Description: Kansas City, MO : Beacon Hill Press of Kansas City, 2016.
Identifiers: LCCN 2016032019 | ISBN 9780834136236 (pbk.)
Subjects: LCSH: Jesus Christ—Knowledge of his own divinity. | Bible. John—Criticism, interpretation, etc. | Jesus Christ—Words.
Classification: LCC BT216.5 .M53 2016 | DDC 232/.8—dc23 LC record available at
https://lccn.loc.gov/2016032019

The internet addresses, email addresses, and phone numbers in this book are accurate at the time of publication. They are provided as a resource. Beacon Hill Press of Kansas City does not endorse them or vouch for their content or permanence.

10 9 8 7 6 5 4 3 2 1

CONTENTS

1

DECLARATION

*Our God comes
and will not be silent;
a fire devours before him,
and around him a tempest rages.*
—Psalm 50:3

God does not stammer. The words are clear, sometimes abrupt, and always with the intent to communicate. In the words of the psalmist, "Our God comes and will not be silent."

The writer of the gospel of John speaks clearly as well. Beginning with the opening words of the gospel, he makes a bold and decisive declaration: "In the beginning was the Word, and the Word was with God, and the Word was God" (1:1). The remainder of the gospel is designed to make an unwavering declaration: *This man Jesus is not just a God-like man. This man is the Son of God!*

The purpose of the declaration is redemption. "But these are written that you may believe that Jesus is the Messiah, the Son of God, and that by believing you may have life in his name" (20:31). It is, therefore, not surprising that throughout the gospel, the writer intends for the reader to see, hear, and experience something of the scandal of his treatise: This Jesus, born of the Virgin Mary, raised as the son of a carpenter in lowly Nazareth, is the very representation of Israel's God, *Yahweh*, the I AM. He is the living, breathing, eating, resting, laughing, weeping demonstration of God in the flesh, come to earth with a redemptive purpose that is clear, visible, accessible, touchable, and intentional.

It is not accidental, therefore, that on many occasions in this gospel Jesus speaks the very utterance that holds the greatest mystery and majesty in the mind and heart of every devout Jew. Twenty-six times in the gospel of John, the Greek words *ego eimi,* "I am," are uttered by Jesus. In some uses of the term, Jesus makes astounding claims that stun the hearers and can even be startling to readers today, even after studying the gospel repeatedly (see 8:56–58).

Seven times the words "I am" are used as a noun with a predicate, designating a particular application of these words to the redemptive mission of Jesus. These seven declarations have been analyzed, studied, and preached since the earliest days following the writing of the gospel of John, and these seven will form the focus of this book.

There are other uses of the words "I am" in the gospel of John that are subtle and easily overlooked but—given the intent of the gospel writer—are not without significance in the overall purpose of the author (see 6:20; 8:24, 28; 13:19). It is necessary to grasp this significant perspective in the fourth gospel. Jesus, altogether and obviously human and accessible, yet speaking with an authority and a depth that often shock his hearers, frequently speaks deferentially of himself. His emphasis is repeatedly and consistently on "the Father who sent me." His purpose, he says, is to reveal the Father and to do his will.

In light of the gospel's pointed emphasis on the many times Jesus expresses this deferential relationship toward the Father, it is fascinating to realize how often, and in so many ways both subtle and direct, the evangelist also records the repeated use by Jesus of the particular and significant term "I am." In order to understand the significance to devout Jews of these two words, and to grasp why hearing Jesus utter them is such a scandal, we must first take a journey backward in time.

Exodus

The hot, burning sands likely shimmer in the heat. The nomadic shepherd is wandering far from his beginning place, searching diligently for adequate grass and available water for his sheep and goats. These flocks and herds are his livelihood. They are the sustenance on which his family and their kin depend for survival. For a nomad, flocks of sheep and herds of goats are the measures of life. Large herds, growing and surviving in the heat and cold of the desert-like land we now call the Middle East, are all that stand between the shepherd's family and utter deprivation.

He has traveled far. Even after four decades of this life, it is never easy to find the best pasture. And he also must remember his immediate family in the search for pasture, water, and safety. It is likely that his travels include his tents, his wife and children, and what other few possessions are necessary to nomadic life. This is security. This is stability. This is home. He has need of nothing more.

It is different this day, though. In the shimmering heat, something startles him, and he turns his head. If there is one thing a shepherd fears, it is fire. Dry grass, brush, and trees can ignite easily and spread quickly in the hot, dry conditions. Dry lightning is an uncontrollable peril. Fire is a mortal threat.

But this day, only a single bush is burning. A bright flame—intense, lasting—and the bush is not being consumed. The fire is not spreading. It is not normal! The shepherd—Moses, he is called—turns aside to look at this strange sight. As he approaches the flaming bush, a voice speaks. It might be as frightening to hear the voice as to see the flame. And the words spoken are terrifying: "Do not come any closer. Take off your sandals, for the place where you are standing is holy ground. I am the God of your father, the God of Abraham, the God of Isaac and the God of Jacob" (portions of Exodus 3:5–6).

We should not wonder that Moses hides his face. This is a moment of encounter with the Divine—filled with mystery, uncertainty, and terror. Suddenly, Moses is hearing a voice from the past. For more than four hundred years his family of origin, the Hebrew people, have lived in Egypt. They came initially as honored guests, the family of a trusted leader among the Egyptian people. They came with an identity as the people of Jacob, who was the father of Joseph—second in command to Pharaoh, king of Egypt. He and his family were followers of the God of Abraham, Isaac, and Jacob.

Over time, their place of honor as welcome guests came into question among the native Egyptians as the rapid growth of the outsiders made the Egyptians increasingly uneasy. The guests eventually became slaves, and the slavery became bitter and oppressive. Destructive edicts requiring extreme measures were issued to limit the further growth of the people of Israel. Male babies were to be killed. The midwives were to become executioners. The Hebrew people cried out to their God, pleading for deliverance, desperate for some kind of response. It no doubt seemed obvious to them that the gods of the Egyptians were stronger than the God of the Hebrews. There was no help. The situation only worsened. Their God, it seemed, had either been bested by the gods of Egypt, or had forgotten them.

But God had not forgotten them. God heard their cries, *experienced* their agony, and made preparations for their deliverance.

Moses seems an unlikely candidate for the mission to which God is calling him. Born a Hebrew during the period when all the male babies were being executed, Moses was rescued by the Egyptian princess and raised in Pharaoh's palace. As such, he was not at home anywhere in Egypt—especially after he killed an Egyptian taskmaster for abusing a Hebrew slave. This incident finally forced him to flee to the wilderness. He ended up in Midian, where he discovered the family of a priest. Here, among descendants of Esau—the other of Isaac's sons—Moses found a place, a home, and a family. He was no longer a stranger in a foreign land.

Now, four decades later, the welfare of the herds and flocks is the purpose around which this shepherd and his people organize their lives. Seeking pasture, water, and safety for the flocks and herds means wandering around vast territories with his family, their tents, and their few belongings. But it is life, and it is normal, and it is often necessary to travel long distances over a period of weeks and months. Having traveled many miles across valleys and through mountain ranges, Moses has, by chance and circumstance, arrived on the slopes of Mount Horeb. That mountain will later hold major significance in the story of God, Moses, and Israel. At this time, however, it is merely the latest place he has come in search of adequate pasture, water, and security for his animals and his family. In the normal routine of caring for these responsibilities, Moses is confronted by the burning bush.

Moses knows God. The people of his birth cry out to this God of their ancestors for deliverance. And Moses has at last found a home among others who know the God of Abraham and Isaac. But Moses has never heard God speak as this God is speaking now. It is stunning. He throws aside his sandals. His body trembles with fear. He covers his face.

The voice speaks: "I have indeed seen the misery of my people in Egypt. I have heard them crying out because of their slave drivers, and I am concerned about their suffering" (3:7). God has not been distant. God is not ignoring their cries. The implication is that God has actually *experienced* their suffering. God is not removed from them. God *feels* their agony, *knows* their misery. And the time has come for God to *act* for their deliverance.

It should not be lost on us that Moses is at the extreme limit of his understanding in this moment. He is overwhelmed, and what he hears is nothing short of terrifying. And it is only natural that Moses seeks to understand *what* he is hearing as well as to know *who* is speaking.

God says to Moses, "So now, go. I am sending you to Pharaoh to bring my people the Israelites out of Egypt" (v. 10).

The exchange between Moses and God is stunning, when we really get into the magnitude of what God is doing and saying to this stammering shepherd. We can easily understand Moses's response to this encounter when he cries out in fear, "Who am I that I should go to Pharaoh and bring the Israelites out of Egypt?" (v. 11).

There is a profound significance that is sometimes overlooked in reading this exchange between God and Moses. Each speaker makes a point to identify himself. Moses cries out, "*Who am I* that *I* should go?"

The response of God is, "*I* will be with you" (v. 12, emphasis added).

Still afraid and uncertain, Moses asks, "What if the Israelites ask me your name? What do I tell them?" (see v. 13). That is not an unexpected question. The Israelites have been slaves in Egypt now for four centuries. The local gods seem obviously dominant, and the pharaoh claims to be of divine descent. What could the God of the Israelites do under these circumstances?

Here, God declares the name by which God will be known to the Israelites from that time forward: "'I AM WHO I AM. This is what you are to say to the Israelites: "I AM has sent me to you."' God also said to Moses, 'Say to the Israelites, "The LORD, the God of your fathers—the God of Abraham, the God of Isaac and the God of Jacob—has sent me to you." This is my name forever, the name you shall call me from generation to generation'" (vv. 14–15).

This is said by some to be the most theological passage in all of Scripture. The significance of the passage in Exodus 3 is not so much the declaration of the *name* of God. It is the revelation and assertion of the *authority* of God. In the very declaration of the name, the authority of the LORD is established.

The LORD: That name is found throughout English translations of the Old Testament, spelled in all capital letters, signifying the utterly holy name by which the Israelites will forever after address or speak of their God. The name is held in such reverence that they hardly dare to speak it aloud. Other descriptive names will be uttered, but that name is held in special reverence.

In Hebrew, the name is *Yahweh.* It has a unique sound that almost should be breathed rather than spoken. And the name, in sound, is drawn from the verb "am" expressed repeatedly, insistently—God declaring the power and authority that only the God of Abraham, Isaac, and Jacob—the Creator of all things—is capable of exercising. The name is given in such a form that every time an Israelite sees the name, thinks the name, or dares to utter the name, it is almost as if he or she is hearing it again: *I AM!*

This is the God who *is*. It would not be enough to say of God that God *was* or *will be*. This is the God who always *is*. This is not *conceptual* being, or being in the abstract. This is active being, present always and everywhere, dynamic and personal being.

Yahweh is not just a name. That name is a *declaration!* Wherever you are in your journey of life, whatever you face in that journey, God *is*. And that is enough.

The Gospel of John and the I Am *Ego Ami*

As compared with the synoptic Gospels (Matthew, Mark, and Luke), the gospel of John is sometimes said to be the spiritual gospel. It would be a mistake to assume that the gospel of John is therefore somewhat less practical and applicable than the others. It would be more appropriate to say that the fourth gospel is written to reveal—to declare—the unique place Jesus has as both Son of Man and Son of God. It takes all four of the Gospels for us to come to the appropriate understanding of all that is meant when we refer to Jesus as Son of God, Son of Man, and Jewish Messiah. But in the fourth gospel, we find the intriguing use of that term of identification that would stir and stun those who would originally read this narrative.

The writer of the fourth gospel has a determined objective. This gospel is written to persuade (John 20:31). And the attempt to persuade is front and center in every chapter and verse. The gospel of John is a gospel of declaration. Among the most stunning means of persuasion is the gospel writer's repeated use of the identifying words on the lips of Jesus: *Ego eimi*.

We must, of course, understand that the words, as Jesus would have spoken them, were likely spoken in Aramaic, the language of the people in the time of Jesus—not Greek. But the Gospels, written decades later, were written in Greek. The Gospels all translate the Aramaic and/or Hebrew language of the life and times of Jesus in Judea and Galilee into Greek, the dominant trade language at the time in which the Gospels were written. Furthermore, the Old Testament in use by the Jews and the Christians in the first century was the Septuagint—the Greek translation of the Hebrew Scriptures. The references and allusions to Old Testament content would be accessible to many, if not most, Jewish people in Greek. Therefore, the gospel uses of the Greek *ego eimi* would be understood for what Jesus intended and for what the writer of the gospel was passionate about communicating.

By the time the gospel of John was written, likely between 85 and 100 CE, the Jewish temple had been destroyed. Great tension began to develop within Judaism, especially between the Pharisaical Jewish leaders and the Christian Jews. With the destruction of the temple, the life of Judaism began to revolve, with even greater significance than before, around the synagogues. Usually formed wherever there were twelve or more Jewish men, the synagogue carried Jewish identity and teaching forward in the absence of that central expression of Judaism that was the temple in Jerusalem.

With the rise of Christianity among the Jewish population, there was an increase in tensions between those who understood and believed Jesus to have been the Jewish Messiah and the Jewish leaders who adamantly opposed such a proposition. These tensions created great anguish for Christian Jews, who were often expelled from the synagogues by the Jewish leaders. It is likely that the purpose for which the gospel of John was originally written was to provide encouragement for the Christians in light of their oppression and persecution by the Jewish leaders.

It is significant that the author of the fourth gospel, writing decades after the events in the life of Jesus about which the gospel is written, makes repeated reference to the use by Jesus of the two words that would stir the attention of Jewish readers and hearers of the text as it was read. The sacred name, on the lips of Jesus, is stunning. And the responses would inevitably be either stunned disbelief and rejection, or breathtaking insight and embrace. Sometimes the writer uses the term in subtle ways. Other times, it is obvious that the intent is to make a bold and undeniable claim of the identity of Jesus as the Son of God, as the revealer of God, as the Jewish Messiah, and as Redeemer of the world.

> *To him who sits on the throne and to the Lamb*
> *be praise and honor and glory and power,*
> *for ever and ever!*
> *—Revelation 5:13*

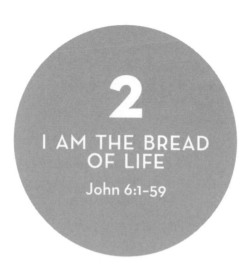

2

I AM THE BREAD OF LIFE

John 6:1–59

Remember how the LORD your God led you all the way in the wilderness . . . to teach you that man does not live on bread alone but on every word that comes from the mouth of the LORD.
—Deuteronomy 8:2–3

The semi-arid land in Jesus's Galilee is often unforgiving and harsh. People have to work to find and prepare food. It is a daily chore that consumes much time for every family. What cannot be planted, cultivated, harvested, and stored during the growing season must be purchased. The population is primarily oriented around subsistence farming, with all able members of the family engaged in the process of growing their crops. The sheep and goats are valued sources of clothing and food but must be carefully tended. The merchants, concentrated in the villages and cities, depend primarily on markets set up for farmers and shepherds to bring their crops and animals to sell. Food is not easily obtained or readily available for anyone.

It is not surprising, then, that Philip becomes uneasy when he sees the growing crowd gathering around and listening to Jesus. They have come hoping to see Jesus perform acts of healing again. Naturally, Philip is astonished that Jesus would think of finding sufficient food to provide a meal for *all* of them. Philip knows that five thousand hungry people could be a problem. He also knows there is no way Jesus and his disciples can find enough money to buy even a morsel for each person—to say nothing of the task of *finding* that much food on a hillside.

It must not be lost on us that the people have gathered around Jesus "because they saw the signs he had performed by healing the sick" (John 6:2). This is not an uninterested crowd. They are following Jesus out of a consuming interest in what he is able to do. There has been conflict between Jesus and some of the religious leaders, but the crowd has seen the miracles. They have come to believe there is something special about Jesus, and they are determined to follow him in hopes of seeing more. Some, no doubt, have brought desperate friends or family members, others struggling to make their way because of their own deep need for healing. A large crowd of people away from home is at serious risk for finding itself without adequate provision for food.

Seeing them gather, Jesus asks Philip, "Where shall we buy bread for these people to eat?" (v. 5).

The response, paraphrased from verse 7, is distressingly predictable: "This is an impossible task! We don't have the necessary resources to meet a need like this!"

Andrew, Simon Peter's brother, brings forward a boy with his small lunch but, with another predictable assertion, says it will certainly not be sufficient to meet the need.

Jesus instructs the disciples to direct the people to be seated on the grassy hillside. Taking the boy's five barley loaves and two small fish, in the hearing and sight of them all, Jesus gives thanks to God. Breaking the bread, he begins to distribute it among the people seated on the grass. Doing the same with the fish, he spreads the food throughout the crowd, providing everyone as much as they want to eat. There is enough left over to fill twelve baskets.

Is it any wonder that the crowd wants to take Jesus by force and make him a king? There are certainly no other kings who can take a boy's small meal and feed thousands! And in a land where finding food is hard work, this is an astounding ability! Crown that man! Though they are willing to make him a king, however, they are not willing to allow him to be what he has actually come to be. It is always hard to recognize God when God refuses to show up in the way we expect.

Knowing their zeal is dangerously misguided, Jesus slips away alone, up into the nearby mountains. The crowds look desperately for him, intent on imposing their will on him, eager to capture his ability for their own purposes.

Toward evening, his disciples make their way to a boat and begin their journey across the lake toward Capernaum. During that journey, Jesus encounters them as they battle the winds and waves of a fierce storm. Already frightened by the storm, they are even more terrified to see someone walking on the water toward them. In the face of their terror, his words are brief but significant—especially given the intent of the writer of this gospel: "It is I [*ego eimi*]; don't be afraid" (v. 20). He joins them in the boat, and "immediately" they arrive at shore (v. 21).

The crowd grows tired of searching for Jesus on the far side of the lake, and when boats become available, many of them make their way to Capernaum in search of Jesus. To their delight, they find him. While wondering when he arrived there—since they watched the disciples get in the boat the previous day and took note that Jesus was not with them—they begin to clamor for him to do it again—to provide more bread. Jesus knows their motivation is misguided and shortsighted. What they want is bread: real, tangible, physical sustenance in a world where providing even a meager amount of bread normally requires work and sacrifice. As important as bread is, that kind of pursuit is not life's highest priority.

This scenario occurs near the Feast of Passover. The people are once again thinking about Moses. In their minds, Moses has no equal. He led the people of Israel in the exodus from Egypt as they escaped the bitterness of their slavery. When they were pursued by Pharaoh's army to the very shores of the Red Sea, Moses led them safely through the waters.

When their food was exhausted, Moses (or so they thought) provided manna and quail in the wilderness. When their throats were parched and dry, Moses brought them water from a rock.

In the series of remarkable events recorded by John in the sixth chapter of his gospel, the exodus is being reinterpreted. One who is greater than Moses is being revealed, and the people are given opportunity to grasp the significance of what they are seeing and hearing. In their clouded minds, it all has to do with his providing *food*—plenty of it, and available for the taking! They are amazed at what Jesus can *do*. But they are utterly oblivious as to *who* he *is*. What should be obvious is lost on them.

Several years ago, three pastors joined me for a night flight in a single-engine aircraft from Phoenix, Arizona, to Albuquerque, New Mexico. It was just dusk when we departed Phoenix Sky Harbor Airport. It was a cloudless evening, and as the darkness deepened, stars carpeted the sky above us. As we flew east at an altitude of 11,500 feet, we could see to the horizon in every direction. Soon, the horizon ahead of us began to take on an orange glow that covered its breadth. I was puzzled by the glow, knowing there was not a large city ahead within a reasonable distance. It looked for a time like fire was spreading widely across the horizon.

We talked about the glow, uncertain about what it indicated. I watched carefully for a few minutes as we flew on, spending time both looking at the brightening glow just at the horizon, and checking my navigational charts in the dim light of the instrument panel.

Soon the glow reached above the horizon and began to take shape as an arch of glowing, iridescent, orange light. It covered fully one half of the horizon ahead of us. In the space of three or four minutes, a sense of awe gripped all of us. We were witnessing the appearance of a full moon, magnified through the atmosphere below and ahead of us. The impact was stunning.

Earlier, I had mentioned to my companions the fact that we would have the advantage of a clear night and a full moon for our flight. I had been expecting to see it. In fact, I was really looking forward to the fact that a full moon would brighten the ground below us with a brilliance none of my passengers could imagine. But I was so prepared for the moon to be bright white, and above us, that I was not prepared for the *appearance* of the moon as it rose from below the horizon ahead of us with a deep-orange color. I saw what I expected to see, but I did not recognize it for what it was. I spent several minutes in uneasy tension as I tried hard to interpret the orange glow that began so subtly and without warning. As we watched the moon slowly rise above the horizon, the orange glow turned to a brilliant white that illuminated the ground below us as if it were daylight.

The hungry crowd of people who saw Jesus feed the five thousand from the small lunch of a young boy saw something that should have captivated them. It ought to have gripped them with a sense of wonder and awe. The words and deeds of Jesus have always been intentional, forthright, and purposeful. But the crowd is blind to what is really happening, in spite of the prophetic writings—in spite of what they have been *expecting*.

Jesus recognizes their blindness. "You are looking for me, not because you saw the signs I performed but because you ate the loaves and had your fill" (v. 26). The gospel writer makes reference to the signs by which Jesus has opened windows into his mission and his identity. Sometimes his words are subtle, his deeds suggesting rather than demanding. But here the intention of Jesus is clear. He is making his identity known in bold deeds and direct words. He presents them with demonstrations of his uniqueness, his authority, his power, and his mission.

Yet they insist that he do things their way. "Do what Moses did," they demand. "Our ancestors ate the manna in the wilderness; as it is written: 'He gave them bread from heaven to eat'" (v. 31). But Jesus turns their words upside down and sets them straight by letting them know that the bread in the wilderness came from God, not from Moses.

Suddenly John makes the essential point of this gospel: Jesus is not just "the prophet." He is much more than a mere miracle worker. The food he provides is not the stuff of magic. In Jesus is the full revelation of God—the ultimate source of life and sustenance. Who he is should be much more important than what he provides. Bread and fish are supposed to direct people's attention to God's new gift—a new Passover/ exodus, led by Jesus, the new Moses. They are being offered access to fullness, to wholeness, to the *shalom* of God, to eternal life, from the hand of God himself. And all they can see is fish and chips.

In John 6, the gospel writer makes clear the irony of this situation. The people of Israel revere Moses. They long for the appearance of "the prophet" to whom Moses referred. The long line of prophets that arose in Israel through the centuries were more often than not ignored, overlooked, resisted, or killed. The people—with whom God has attempted to speak clearly and directly through the prophets—have heard the very word of God, and missed it! And now, insists the gospel writer, the "prophet like Moses," the fulfillment of all that the previous prophets have spoken, stands in their presence, and the people are missing it again!

Jesus challenges their pursuit of bread and fish. God's gift is "true bread," he says (v. 32). "For the bread of God is the bread that comes down from heaven and gives life to the world" (v. 33). People who are hungry for bread are not *necessarily* blind to greater realities. It is just so hard to sort out the priorities. But the words of Jesus strike home. Now they begin, at least in some measure, to recognize the greater value of which Jesus speaks: "'Sir,' they said, 'always give us *this* bread'" (v. 34, emphasis added).

In a final appeal to them to recognize who stands before them, Jesus says in the very clearest of terms, "I am the bread of life. Whoever comes to me will never go hungry, and whoever believes in me will never be thirsty" (v. 35). As Jesus continues, the crowd grows restless and argumentative. His words confuse them, given their unwillingness to grasp the significance of what they have seen and heard.

In a world where the tangible, the physical, or the visible represent reality for so many, it is often difficult to grapple with spiritual meanings and priorities. But the words of Jesus drive more deeply into his meaning, providing greater access to the depths of his mission in the world. But the people only argue more vigorously among themselves. Jesus attempts over and over to direct them away from the primacy of pursuing bread that temporarily fills the stomach in favor of consuming the bread that will feed them life everlasting. Jesus challenges their blindness to his mission with the invitation and the promise that, if they eat the bread that comes down from heaven, they will live and not die.

Though the initiation of the Eucharist is not related to us in the gospel of John, it is clear that what Jesus says to the hungry seekers in Capernaum is intended to convey to the reader of this gospel the deep significance of that observance. In words that prefigure the initiation of the Lord's Supper, he invites them to "eat the flesh of the Son of Man and drink his blood" (v. 53). Jesus says his flesh and blood are real food and drink (v. 55). In doing so, he gives to us today insight into what he was attempting to reveal to the crowds around him. In this light, the significance of the Lord's Supper begins to take on new meaning for Christians today.

Just before his betrayal and all that follows, Jesus meets with his disciples in the upper room. In that setting, they observe the Passover celebration by eating a meal whose menu includes items that are filled with symbolic reminders of the exodus. The Passover meal is the defining religious observance for the Jews. Just as his disciples are preparing to eat the unleavened bread required in the Passover meal, Jesus takes the bread and, after giving thanks (the Greek word for "thanks" is the word from which we get the term *Eucharist* [Luke 22:17]), breaks it and distributes it to his disciples. He says to them, "This is my body given for you; do this in remembrance of me" (Luke 22:19). After the meal, he lifts the cup of wine, another reminder of the Passover, and says to them, "This cup is the new covenant in my blood, which is poured out for you" (Luke 22:20).

Suddenly, old forms and observances have entirely new impact. Old traditions that have become stale and probably often meaningless are replaced with new significance, meaning, and hope. Here is a new exodus. This is the new Passover. No longer is an intermediary (such as Moses) the agent through whom God makes provision for God's people. Now the provision is available through the extended hand of God's own self through the Son!

When Jesus says, "I am the bread of life" in John 6, it is in fervent hope that the people who saw the miracle of the feeding of the five thousand will grasp the wonder that, in Jesus, God has begun the final and decisive chapter in the redemption of the world. The purposes for which Israel was raised up and chosen are now coming to fruition in the Son of God. "Whoever comes to me will never go hungry, and whoever believes in me will never be thirsty" (v. 35).

With this understanding, when we take the bread into our hands in celebration of the Lord's Supper, our hearts begin to beat with new hope. While that morsel of bread is not sufficient to silence the growling of an empty stomach, it does point to a grand reality far more significant than mere bread. God has come to earth in the Son. "Food that endures to eternal life" (v. 27) is ours. Redemption for humanity is underway. The kingdom of God has begun.

> Come, all you who are thirsty,
> come to the waters;
> and you who have no money,
> come, buy and eat!
> Come, buy wine and milk
> without money and without cost.
> Why spend money on what is not bread,
> and your labor on what does not satisfy?
> Listen, listen to me, and eat what is good,
> and you will delight in the richest of fare.
> —Isaiah 55:1–2

3

I AM THE LIGHT OF THE WORLD

John 8:12-20; 9:1-25

For with you is the fountain of life;
in your light we see light.
—Psalm 36:9

If you were going to create the universe, where would you begin? In the Genesis account of creation, the first day of creation ends only after light has been created. In our finite understanding of the creation epic, it is difficult to imagine what it must have been like before light. For most of us, darkness is never total. Light bleeds into our lives even in the darkness because it is almost impossible to be any place where there is not *some* evidence of light. If we do find ourselves in total darkness, it is disorienting and disturbing.

Several years ago my wife, Susan, and I visited a cavern in the Smoky Mountains area of the U.S. There were about a dozen tourists with us as we made our way deep into the cavern along a rough pathway. Dim lights guided us to the final location of our tour, where we entered a large, open space, a huge room within the cavern. After some descriptions of the size of the cavern and its place in both the geological history of the area and in human history, our guide asked each of us to place our hands on the rail near which we all stood. Then he turned off all the lights in that deep cavern. There was not a trace of light. The darkness was thick and overpowering. It suddenly became obvious why he had asked us to place our hands on the rail. The floor was slightly uneven, tilting. If you removed your hand from the rail, you had no reference as to what was level. A disorienting sense of imbalance crept over you. I remember holding Susan's hand and noticing her grip getting tighter. She had removed her hand from the rail and was unable to relocate it in the darkness. It was a relief to all of us when the guide turned on a small flashlight. In that deep darkness, the tiny light seemed brilliant! We were glad, too, when *all* the lights came back on.

Since that stunning moment when God said, "Let there be light!" light has come to signify not only the ability of God to create from nothing but also the very character and being of God.

Israel's scribes and teachers long understood light as an essential descriptor of the being and character of God.

"The LORD is my light and my salvation," sang David in Psalm 27:1.

"The LORD will be your everlasting light," cried Isaiah (60:19).

"By his light I walked through darkness!" insisted Job (29:3).

In summarizing his hope in spite of the darkness and despair he saw all around him, Micah faced the future with hope: "Though I sit in darkness, the LORD will be my light. . . . He will bring me out into the light; I will see his righteousness" (7:8, 9).

Israel's mission, from the beginning, was clear. They were to be the chosen people of God, through whom God would reveal the light of love and mercy to the entire world. But the story of Israel across the scope of Old Testament history reveals how utterly they failed to fulfill this vital mission. Blinded by their sin and stubborn willfulness, Israel insisted on crafting God after their own image and, in doing so, participated in disseminating darkness and death rather than light and life.

The prophet Isaiah grasped the revelation that there would be a "servant" of God, a messiah who would fulfill the mission for which the nation of Israel was chosen. The Servant would "bring justice to the nations" and be a light to the Gentiles. He would "open eyes that are blind" and shine a light for "those who sit in darkness" (42:1, 6, 7).

It is the full intent of the writer of the gospel of John to present Jesus as that servant of God, the Messiah. His carefully crafted narrative reaches into the prophetic memory of Israel, drawing on images that the Old Testament writers used repeatedly. Among those images is the one of God as light and life. As John opens his narrative, the first verses make clear that Jesus—the Word of God—is light and life.

Light Revealed and Challenged (John 8:12-20)

In another of the "I am" sayings woven into John's account, we are given a bold claim that what God was to Israel, and what Israel was intended to be to the world, Jesus *is.* The setting for Jesus calling himself the light of the world is during the Feast of Tabernacles, one of the major annual feasts for the Jews.

The Feast of Tabernacles was a joyous celebration. On the first night of the celebration, four large lampstands were placed in the Court of the Women. The light from these lampstands was so brilliant that court-yards across the city reflected it. In addition, celebrants carrying burning torches danced before the lampstands, adding even more brilliance to the evening. Some of the celebrants spilled out into the city around the temple with their torches. Each night during the festival the lamps were lit, the brilliance mesmerized the people, and every resident of Jerusalem was touched by light.

The lighting of the lamps was one of two daily ceremonies during the Feast of Tabernacles, each intended to point the minds of the celebrants to the miraculous deliverance of Israel from slavery in Egypt and to God's faithful presence and provision during the forty years of wandering in the wilderness. In the early morning, at the time of the daily sacrifice, a priest filled a pitcher with water drawn from the Pool of Siloam. The water was to be poured out as a drink offering, reminding the people that God provided water from the rock when they were desperately thirsty. The ceremony was a moment of celebration and joy, and people cheered and praised God, quoting the Hallel Psalms (113–118) as the priest poured out the water and then lifted his hand as a signal that the water had been offered as praise to God.

It is perhaps at this moment, on one of the climactic days of the festival, that Jesus cries out, "Let anyone who is thirsty come to me and drink" (7:37). It must be like a thunderclap! Those who hear him do not question the implication of his words. This is a bold, unequivocal claim: *What this symbol proclaims, I am.* The immediate response is division. Some wonder. Some condemn. But some believe.

It may well be that, in participating in the feasting, dancing, and singing that accompany the Feast of Tabernacles, the people have come to dissociate the celebration from the intended meaning of the festival. It is dangerous when symbols that are intended to point to a greater reality become a substitute for the reality itself. What was intended as a reminder of the pillar of fire that guided and guarded the people of Israel during the exodus and the forty years of wilderness wanderings has become distorted in the fervor of bright flames, dancing, and feasting.

While the people celebrate in the light of the lampstands and the torches, basking in the light, and little realizing the intended significance of their celebration, Jesus cries out to the crowd, "I am the light of the world!" (8:12). For those who hear him, it must be a stunning moment.

Immediately, the Pharisees challenge his words. Standing on their own assumptions of superior knowledge and understanding, they cannot tolerate anyone who serves as their own witness as the basis of assumed authority. You can almost hear them saying, in words familiar to many of us today, "Who do you think you *are?*"

The Pharisees stand on what was a common legal necessity in Israel. No man can witness to himself. Any claim to right or truth by an individual must have the verification of at least two other witnesses. The basis of such a requirement is the inherent suspicion that people are too self-interested to be trusted as witnesses to their own cause.

It is interesting to note what John is doing in this passage. He has already made it clear who Jesus is. He uses the encounter with the Pharisees to demonstrate how utterly unaware *they* are as to his true identity. Their judgments are based on the flesh—on merely human categories, totally devoid of the willingness to grasp what Jesus is doing and saying. Even so, Jesus plays by their rules. *Need a second witness to be satisfied?* Jesus asks them. *Okay, you've got it*: "In your own Law it is written that the testimony of two witnesses is true. I am one who testifies for myself; my other witness is the Father, who sent me" (8:17–18). Here is one of the grand moments of insight into John's gospel. It is said by some that the central figure in the gospel of John is not Jesus but, rather, "the Father, who sent me." It is interesting to see the continual references made by Jesus to his Father. These are not incidental; they are at the very heart of his self-disclosure: "I am not here on my own authority, but he who sent me is true" (7:28).

The Pharisees' demand for a verifying witness is evidence of their utter blindness to Jesus's true identity. "If you knew me," he says, "you would know my Father also" (8:19). It is here that our own reading of the gospel of John may be at the greatest risk. If we miss the point of what the writer intends to convey, we will find ourselves commiserating with the opponents of Jesus, affirming their demand that he not be allowed to serve as his own witness. But the gospel writer will have none of that! This is the Son of Man. He has come from the Father. There can be no greater witness to his identity, and to his relation to the Father, than his own word. If they could only grasp who this is, his word would be enough!

Darkness Confronted and Defeated (John 9:1–12)

John gives us one of the most graphic demonstrations of Jesus's efforts to open the minds of the Pharisees and others watching Jesus with deep suspicion. Blinded by their own prejudices and preconceptions, they cannot see Jesus for who he is. As if to make their blindness obvious and visible, both to themselves and to others, the gospel writer recounts Jesus's encounter with a man who was born blind.

We should not find it difficult to understand the questions the disciples raise in the face of unexplained blindness. How could this man, who has been blind from birth, be guilty of a sin that would have resulted in his blindness? In response, Jesus challenges the disciples with a jarring truth: Speculations regarding the cause of the blindness are a distraction from the mission of the disciples, then and now: "As long as it is day, we must do the works of him who sent me. Night is coming, when no one can work. While I am in the world, I am the light of the world" (9:4–5).

A critically important insight into the understanding of salvation from sin is found at this point in the gospel of John. While, for many, the scope and nature of sin are related to transgressing the law, it is the purpose of this gospel to make clear that—prior to grasping the importance of the death of Jesus as expiation for violating the law—sin must be seen as refusing to acknowledge the identity and mission of Jesus. For this gospel, the blindness of not recognizing who Jesus is and the darkness of refusing to believe in him are categories of sin, chosen in lieu of belief in Jesus as the revelation of God.

To John, the darkness that is chosen is the deepest darkness. To not believe in Jesus is evidence not of inability but of unwillingness, of refusal to see. Jesus, the one sent by the Father, is the perfect representation of the Father. He is God in the flesh, making clear and accessible all that God is and desires to do. The very refusal to see, to believe, seals the darkness for those who oppose and challenge Jesus at every turn. This is why the description of the healing of the man born blind is so central to understanding the objective of the gospel of John. With a deliberation not seen in some of his miracles, Jesus spits on the ground and makes some mud with the saliva. He places it on the man's eyes. He then instructs the man to go and wash in the Pool of Siloam. This pool is traditionally understood as the one from which the waters are taken for use in the celebration of the Feast of Tabernacles, linking this healing miracle to the celebration and to the encounters with the Pharisees in the previous chapter. When the man washes the mud from his eyes, he can see!

That he can see is the pivotal metaphor. Jesus says in verse 5: "While I am in the world, I am the light of the world." Having now provided sight, light, and revelation, Jesus stands before the man, the disciples, and the Pharisees as the ultimate revelation of God. To see Jesus is to see the Father.

Faith Awakened and Victorious (John 9:13-25)

That the "work" of kneading the mud and placing it on the man's eyes is done on the Sabbath only deepens the hostility of the Pharisees. Their anger is immediate and their suspicion strong. "This man is not from God," they insist, "for he does not keep the Sabbath" (v. 16).

The man who was born blind can now see, and the Pharisees who claim they can see are even more blind than they know! The continuing encounter with the man who was blind becomes a demonstration of the power of darkness. What may be for some unbelief soon becomes for others refusal to believe, even in the face of overwhelming evidence. The refusal to believe soon demands that the evidence itself be done away with. They throw the man who has been given his sight out of the synagogue.

When light encounters darkness, conflict is inevitable. However, in a moment of tender encounter after the man is thrown out of the synagogue, Jesus reveals himself as the light that lifts blindness—both physically and spiritually. But those who think that by their judgments they can reject the claims of Jesus as the light of the world find themselves under a judgment they cannot escape.

A few years ago I suffered an eye injury that made it necessary to wear a medicated patch over one eye for several days. The eye slowly healed, and the day came for the patch to be removed and the eye given the chance to begin to adjust to light. After several days of darkness, the light was jarring on that eye. I complained to the doctor that the injury was not sufficiently healed and that wearing the patch a bit longer might be wise. His response was immediate: "Oh, no. That would be unwise. The eye must adjust to the light. It will be sensitive, even painful, for a while, but don't cover the eye. Don't keep it closed. Expose the eye to the light and allow the light to continue the work of healing the wound."

The wound of sin is blindness to the light of the world. The spirit of humanity is accustomed to the darkness. It even relishes the darkness, celebrates it, and seeks to embrace it. But it is the work of the Spirit of Christ to bring light, sometimes painfully, and always with a piercing intent to do away with the darkness of sin and unbelief. In that light, we must embrace the clear, unwavering insistence of Jesus: "I am the light of the world."

Arise, shine, for your light has come,
and the glory of the LORD rises upon you.
See, darkness covers the earth
and thick darkness is over the peoples,
but the LORD rises upon you
and his glory appears over you.
Nations will come to your light,
and kings to the brightness of your dawn.
—Isaiah 60:1-3

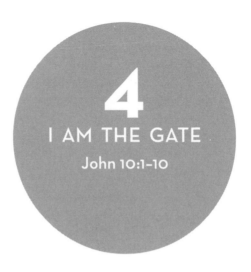

4

I AM THE GATE

John 10:1–10

Enter his gates with thanksgiving
and his courts with praise;
give thanks to him and praise his name.
—Psalm 100:4

The tenth chapter of the gospel of John is filled with a rich array of images, figures of speech, metaphors, and analogies. It is complex in its arrangement and sometimes difficult to interpret. However, discerning the meaning of Jesus's words is central to an understanding of the person and mission of Jesus and what it means to be part of the community of faith. The problem we often have is like that of the Jewish religious leaders, whose imaginations are starved by their intense hatred of Jesus. By their stubborn and willful unbelief, they are blind to the reality that stands before them.

This chapter immediately follows the conflict with the Pharisees over the healing of the man born blind. The reader of this section of the gospel is brought into the dialogue as an observer and an interpreter. In the brilliant structure of the written material, truth begins to seep through the narrative, engaging the reader at several levels. It is possible to find yourself so caught up in the story that you can take part in the dialogue, identifying with one or another of the characters. It then becomes possible to begin drawing conclusions never fully stated in the narrative but obvious nonetheless. As the Pharisees pursue Jesus with increasing animosity, it becomes clear that there is a fatal blindness. Jesus boldly confronts their blindness in the discourse and through the images of the sheep, the shepherd, the sheep pen, and the gate.

The image of the shepherd is a familiar one in Israel's long story. Leaders of Israel have often been referred to as shepherds. God has been spoken of as the shepherd of Israel (Psalms 23, 100). Pastoral imagery resonates with the people of this culture. Shepherds are a common sight, and their work is essential to the economic, religious, and physical well-being of the people.

But images of shepherds who neglect their responsibilities are also common in Jewish writings and stories. Frequent references are found in the prophetic writings of the shepherds of Israel who neglect their flocks, who exploit them for personal gain, or who abandon them in times of danger (Jeremiah 50:6–7; Zechariah 11, Ezekiel 34:7–10).

In parts of the Middle East to this day, shepherds are a common sight. Herds of sheep or goats are seen scattered across the barren land, their shepherds watching closely, usually walking among them or sitting nearby. Their work is hard, often requiring long periods of isolation. In the more remote areas, they lead the herds across rocky fields and craggy hills seeking water, grass, and other growth to provide necessary sustenance. Sometimes the animals are thin—evidence of the barrenness of the landscape. Most of the sheep are kept for their ability to produce wool. The tangled, long, shaggy coats are valuable resources for their shepherds, and the care of the flock is essential to the welfare of the shepherd's family.

In the more populated areas, near villages or towns, herds of sheep are often kept in common folds or pens at night, with a guard or shepherd watching the gate, carefully attending the fold, and allowing entrance only to those shepherds whose sheep are in that fold. A thief or robber who attempts to enter is likely one for whom the long-term care of the animals is not a value. The purpose of thievery is more likely to kill the animal for food or to sell its wool.

The Parable (10:1-4)

The conflict with the Pharisees revolves around the identity of Jesus. Where did he come from? Where did he get the authority with which he speaks? How did those miracles occur? Is he from God? Is he the long-awaited Messiah—or not? In the ongoing conflict, the Pharisees are intent on disproving or challenging any suggestion that Jesus might possibly be far more than they are willing to see or understand. Blinded by their own insistence that any purported Messiah conform to their preconceptions of what to expect, they grow more and more frustrated by their inability to put an end to the pretensions of this disturbing teacher and healer.

Jesus well knows their frustration and is the target of their caustic criticisms and increasing threats. In response he speaks candidly, challenging their inadequate knowledge of what they claim to know so thoroughly. Seeing how their blindness to the truth is leading the people astray, Jesus challenges them with several metaphors and analogies that are intended to make clear the dangers and risks their blindness presents to themselves and to the people who are influenced by them.

The prophet Jeremiah spoke to rebellious Israel in 5:21, referring to those "who have eyes but do not see, who have ears but do not hear." The proverb often found in song and script, "there are none so blind as those who will not see," applies to the Jewish leaders. And even yet, Jesus makes appeal after appeal, invitation after invitation, to the stumbling, stubborn leaders.

The story with which this chapter opens is much more than a parable. It has the traditional characteristics of a parable but probes deeper and with greater intent than we might see on the surface. The author of the gospel calls it a "figure of speech" (John 10:6). In it, Jesus uses several images to make his point. It is a waste of time and energy to try to interpret every image as having equal significance. Some of the images serve as props while others carry the weight of the lesson he seeks to teach.

In this passage, for instance, he speaks of robbers and thieves. Anyone who enters a sheep pen by any other means than the gate is up to no good! Because of their stubborn refusal to be open to who Jesus is, they have become obstacles to God's mission of mercy and redemption. As a result, Jesus levels a stern warning about robbers.

The Problem (John 10:5-6)

The Pharisees claim to be Israel's spiritual leaders. They claim to be the guardians of orthodoxy, but they jealously guard their place, often seeking to balance the demands of the Jewish Law as they interpret it, and the myriad regulations they impose, against the demands of the occupying Roman government. It is not an easy effort. Their tenuous grasp on power as religious leaders is under constant threat from the pagan Romans, as well as under constant pressure from the Jewish people. The Jews, oppressed both religiously and militarily, are in a state of constant turmoil and dissatisfaction. As a result, as is seen in many places in the Gospels, the Pharisees and other leaders of the Jews are often protective of their own interests, at the expense of the integrity of their role as Israel's spiritual leaders. They are so blinded by their own preoccupations and agendas they cannot see God standing before them in Jesus.

The study of the history of royal succession in Israelite history is fascinating—and convoluted. The kings of Israel—all of them successors to the ideal king, David—were intended to represent the very presence of God among the people. They were to lead under the direction of the LORD, and their role as shepherds over the flock of God was a primary responsibility. By the time of Jesus, the legitimacy of succession has been lost during the centuries of rebellious disobedience, exile, and domination by other empires. The Jewish high priest and the religious leaders of the Jewish people are claimants to the right to rule and are, in many ways, pretenders to the throne and to the responsibilities of spiritual leadership.

There is another fascinating study of pretenders to various thrones or empires in our own time. There are people who themselves, or in a few cases, others on behalf of them, make claims to be the rightful heirs of thrones that no longer exist. In some cases, kings were overthrown, or the ruler abdicated the throne, and other types of government were established. Those who are descendants of those who were overthrown, on occasion, make claims that they are still the legitimate leaders of those kingdoms or nations. But while they may make the claims—and, in some cases, can prove their lineage—those kingdoms no longer exist, and their claims to authority and power are without merit.

But spiritual leadership demands more than preoccupation with selfish ambition, self-protection, or a grasping for power and position. Godly leadership is appropriately ambitious, but it is a selfless ambition. The objectives of godly leadership are worship, the advancement of the kingdom of God, and the redemption of all people—the very reasons Jesus came into the world. These objectives are the basis for the challenge he issues to the Pharisees. Their exercise of leadership is arrogant, sometimes arbitrary, and often authoritarian. The problem, however, is that they are, in reality, pretenders to the role of spiritual leadership. Jesus, the legitimate descendant of King David, speaks with authority but never in arrogance. He is compassionate, and he is capable of discerning particular needs among the people who flock to him, but he is never arbitrary in the exercise of his leadership. He is the Shepherd who laid down his life for the sheep.

The Promise (John 10:7-10)

While this passage certainly offers essential guidance for the exercise of appropriate leadership in both the business world of today and in the church of Jesus Christ, it also challenges the arrogance of any who would seek to determine who is in or out of the kingdom of God by their own authority. Those determinations do not belong to people who seek to exercise spiritual authority on the basis of privilege or position. In the previous chapter, the Pharisees threw out of the synagogue the man who was born blind, to whom Jesus gave sight. Seeing what happened, Jesus found the man and gave him a place in the kingdom. In this passage Jesus speaks with divine authority when he says, "I am the gate for the sheep. All who have come before me are thieves and robbers" (vv. 7–8).

The primary issue here is not how leadership is selected or how leadership should be exercised so much as the clear and unequivocal basis of entrance into the kingdom for every person. There is one way—and only one—by which access is granted into the kingdom. Jesus makes that abundantly clear when he says, "I am the gate; whoever enters through me will be saved" (v. 9).

God has been reconciled to God's creation. The way is open for all humanity to enter into relationship with God. Jesus—the perfect representation of the very nature and character of God—has broken down the dividing wall of hostility that existed between God and humanity.

Once again Jesus draws a stunning contrast between the Pharisees' failure to exercise their role as Israel's spiritual leaders and his role as the gate: "The thief comes only to steal and kill and destroy; I have come that they may have life, and have it to the full" (v. 10).

No more graphic distinction can be shown. While there is no doubt that there are some among the religious leaders of the day who are genuine seekers after the truth (Nicodemus, for example, in John 3), the weight of their grasp on power is leveraged against Jesus and his mission. So threatened are they by his mission and message that they are blind to the outcomes of their rage and opposition: "The thief comes only to steal and kill and destroy." They are unwilling and unable to see the damage they are doing, and it is indeed damaging beyond what they can imagine. However, they are also so blind to reality that they are incapable of understanding the ultimate expression of the authority of Jesus: "I have come that they may have life, and have it to the full."

Their power and authority are rendered futile and irrelevant on that first Easter morning. The resurrection is the masterstroke of God, the final measure of authority and power, and is exercised as a rebuke to all other pretensions of power and authority.

"Who do you think you are?!" they rage.

"I am the gate," he says. "Through me, and only through me, you find life!"

> *But now, this is what the LORD says—*
> *he who created you, Jacob,*
> *he who formed you, Israel:*
> *"Do not fear, for I have redeemed you;*
> *I have summoned you by name; you are mine.*
>
> *For I am the LORD your God,*
> *the Holy One of Israel, your Savior."*
> *—Isaiah 43:1, 3a*

5

I AM THE GOOD SHEPHERD

John 10:11-21

He who scattered Israel will gather them
and will watch over his flock like a shepherd.
—Jeremiah 31:10

Exile is a bitter pill to swallow. The trauma, the incoherence, the dislocation all contribute to a sense of abandonment, betrayal, and profound, irretrievable loss. The prophet Ezekiel spoke into that swirl of tangled emotion and grief with a message few wanted to hear. It was confusing, often incoherent in its own right, and seldom gave any sense of hope. It was like a dagger, piercing deep into the soul of the exiles: "You reap what you sow!" *You should not be surprised,* he seemed to say. *This is the outcome of callous disregard for the holiness of God. This is the harvest of profligate living, self-absorbed worship, and empty ritual.*

The exiles had been away from home some ten years, and to add to their grief and despair came news that Jerusalem had fallen, its walls torn down, the temple desecrated and destroyed. All hope of redemption was gone.

"But you are not abandoned," said Ezekiel. "The God of your fathers has not forgotten you. Your God has not turned away from you.

If you will see it, God's sovereign majesty is at work around you, among you, and within you." Carefully, graphically, and with deep conviction, the prophet painted a picture of the unseen hand of God, working on their behalf, altering the affairs of nations, reversing the fortunes of kings and generals. "God knows where you are," said the prophet. "And God is at work in ways both seen and unseen."

Into that maelstrom, words of hope and assurance began to pour into the hearts and minds of the exiles in Babylon. "I myself will be the shepherd of my sheep, and I will make them lie down, says the Lord GOD. I will seek the lost, and I will bring back the strayed, and I will bind up the injured, and I will strengthen the weak" (Ezekiel 34:15–16a, NRSV).

One of the most enduring images in the Christian faith is the image of the Good Shepherd. It is embedded in our memories, depicted in our art, and displayed in our homes and churches. One of the most beloved psalms is the twenty-third, read and quoted in times of both joy and sorrow. The words resonate deeply in the memories of many Christians. Millions have seen Warner Sallman's painting depicting Jesus as a shepherd, surrounded by a dozen or more sheep, one of them black, and carrying a lamb in his arms.

The words of Jesus in John 10 have been a source of comfort and assurance for believers from the earliest centuries of the Christian era. It is significant that the term *pastor* in the context of the church is taken from the Latin root that means *shepherd*. This concept is woven deeply into the Christian tradition, as well it should be.

Jesus utters these memorable words in the context of sharp debate between himself and the Pharisees. He has exercised his pastoral concern in giving sight to a man born blind (John 9). His critics are offended that this event occurred on the Sabbath, yet they are confounded by the miracle of healing. But unable and unwilling to accept what they are observing through eyes of faith and hope, they become enraged enough to finally throw the man who was healed out of the synagogue.

Jesus does not casually toss out the words he expresses in John 10:11–18. He and all his hearers are aware of the image he draws out before them. The prophet Ezekiel spoke words of harsh condemnation for the kings and religious leaders of Israel who plundered and abused the people of God. Now, as Jesus confronts the Pharisees and other religious leaders, his words are no mystery to them. It is obvious to everyone that Jesus's meaning is directed toward the very people who stand before him. Not much has changed. Callous, indifferent, self-serving religious leaders are blinding the people to who stands before them. Despite his repeated miracles, deliverances, and sermons, they still refuse to acknowledge him for who he is.

Since early in his ministry, Jesus has been carefully but persistently confronting the spiritual blindness of the Pharisees and other religious leaders—the blind guides of the Jewish people. He does so fully understanding his role as the Shepherd of Israel and no doubt reflecting on the images contained in Ezekiel 34. In that well-known passage the Lord spoke words of assurance to scattered and broken Israel: "I myself will search for my sheep and look after them" (v. 11).

The contrast between what happened to the man born blind and what Jesus says of his own mission and purpose is stunning. The Pharisees are angry and confused. They react with bitter accusations and condemnation, only deepening the obvious gulf between their conduct and his mission.

The Good Shepherd Protects the Sheep (John 10:11-13)

Few of us today would miss the implication of Jesus's words when he speaks of the good shepherd laying down his life for the sheep. The benefit of two thousand years of Christian tradition and knowledge lead us to a rather quick assumption that the reference is to the cross. While that is true, and should not be overlooked, it can easily slip by us that the shepherd who is deeply invested in his or her task has made a life choice in the very act of *becoming* a shepherd. The choice to follow this calling leads shepherds to make of their lives a "living sacrifice" (Romans 12:1). One whose task is to care for wandering and vulnerable sheep has little time for anything else. For the shepherd to whom the sheep belong, these creatures are more than a commodity. Caring for these sheep is more than a job. These animals are the source of life and sustenance for the shepherd and his family. He dare not approach his task as a hireling, whose primary interest is mere monetary compensation. This is an investment of the shepherd's life, and this kind of care demands great risk of the shepherd. Wolves, lions, and thieves are occupational hazards that cannot be avoided for the true shepherd.

Jesus sees in the attitudes and actions of the Pharisees a fundamental violation of the very purpose for which they are supposed to be engaged in their role as Israel's shepherds. The challenge that Jesus issues to the Pharisees is not mean-spirited or capricious. His concern for the sheep—for the people of Israel—is so all encompassing that any risk to the welfare of the sheep demands a forthright confrontation with the source of the danger.

Echoes of the words of Ezekiel reverberate through the words of Jesus. The prophet poured out his heart in anguish, conveying the words of God on behalf of the stunned and grieving exiles in Babylon. *You shepherds have only taken care of yourselves*, cried the prophet (see 34:2). "You have not strengthened the weak or healed the sick or bound up the injured. You have not brought back the strays or searched for the lost. You have ruled them harshly and brutally" (v. 4).

Jesus's confrontation with the religious leaders of his day reveals once again the danger and destructiveness of an arrogant and self-serving religiosity that can so subtly characterize the practice of ministry in the name of God.

But we must not forget that Jesus is just as quick to embrace those Pharisees who genuinely seek the truth (John 3:1–21; 19:38–42) as he is to challenge the motives and practices of those who refuse to see the Truth when he appears.

The Good Shepherd Knows the Sheep (John 10:14–16)

There is hardly a more gracious statement found in this passage than "I know my sheep and my sheep know me" (John 10:14). That phrase is packed with meaning, especially for those who understand the relationship between a shepherd and the sheep.

Most shepherds have a knack for knowing the particular characteristics of individual sheep. They often have names for them, like Black Ear, Blue Eye, Skipper. The shepherd knows what terrain is most threatening to some of the sheep and will watch those few even more carefully when leading the flock through a rugged area posing certain threats. Sheep become so accustomed to the voice of their shepherd that, even were another person to know their names, the sheep can detect and will obey only the particular voice of their own shepherd. Some stories are told about shepherds in the Middle East who play hand-carved, wooden flutes. Even if some other shepherd gets that flute, the tones, cadences, and rhythms of each shepherd are unique enough that the sheep will only follow when their own shepherd plays. Some sheep are said to "dance" to the tune of their shepherd as they are called to follow.

The prophet Ezekiel understood the intimate and attentive relationship of the shepherd with the sheep. God spoke through the prophet to comfort the exiles with these words: "I myself will search for my sheep and look after them. As a shepherd looks after his scattered flock when he is with them, so will I look after my sheep. . . . I myself will tend my sheep and have them lie down, declares the Sovereign LORD" (Ezekiel 34:11b–12a, 15).

The Good Shepherd Confronts the Dangers (John 10:17–21)

All of this information about sheep and shepherds is fascinating and may hold some interest for today's reader as a means of understanding the setting in which Jesus lives his life in Judea and Galilee. But it is essential to note a shift in the way Jesus speaks in this passage. He begins to move from analogy to personal application. He begins to make claims that confront the Pharisees again with the unique relationship he has with the Father, with Israel, and with the wider world of the Gentiles.

This is one of the most stunning and radical statements that Jesus has made to this point. He no longer relies on figures of speech, parables, or analogies. "The Father knows me and I know the Father," he says (John 10:15). It is little wonder that the writer says, "The Jews who heard these words were again divided" (v. 19). These are not veiled words, and they are not spoken timidly or with reserve. The Lord of creation speaks on the basis of his relationship with the Father. The hearers must make a determination about how they hear the words. Will they hear them with skepticism and doubt or with faith and wonder? The dividing line is still the same. How do we hear these words today?

Further, the words challenge the narrow and exclusivist perspective of the Pharisees who seem to ignore the mission given to Abraham— whose people were to be a light to the nations. They are *supposed* to bring the Gentiles into the fold! The Pharisees see outsiders as threatening and devalued. They are not *us*. They do not belong. But Jesus is not willing to allow that perspective to go unchallenged. While the Pharisees are kicking people out of the synagogues, the mission of Jesus is to open the gates of the kingdom of God to all comers. "I have other sheep that are not of this sheep pen," he says. "I must bring them also. They too will listen to my voice, and there shall be one flock and one shepherd" (v. 16).

To hardened hearts and furious opponents, Jesus speaks with candor, conviction, and resolve. He will not be deterred, even in the face of their threats and accusations: "He is demon-possessed and raving mad," they say about him (v. 20). Knowing that they are beginning to plot to kill him, he challenges their authority with a conviction that can come only when you know who you are and on whose authority you have come. "The reason my Father loves me," he says, "is that I lay down my life—only to take it up again" (v. 17). That phrase is packed with deep and profound meaning. His suffering and death are not accidents of circumstance, nor are they the successful accomplishment of those who plot his death. Jesus makes it abundantly clear that his efforts are intentional, his control of the outcome complete, and the success of his mission assured.

In a world where the power of evil seems rampant and unchallenged, it is instructive for Christians in the twenty-first century to stand on this assurance: The mission of God *is* advancing. The appearances to the contrary are just that—appearances. Though evil is pervasive, it is not ultimate. Though sin ravages and destroys, it is not victorious. Though battles are hard-fought, and setbacks do occur, the final victory of Jesus Christ is a certainty that will not die.

Jesus declares his authority to both lay his life down *and* to take it up again. The suffering death and resurrection of Jesus Christ are the foundations for our hope. We have no reason to be timid or shy in our proclamation of this wonderful truth. It may be that certain cousins of the Pharisees will scoff and belittle, but the Good Shepherd reigns. Those who seek to steal, kill, and destroy will ultimately fail in their endeavors. The promise is secure, and the prospect is exciting beyond description: "I have come that they may have life, and have it to the full" (v. 10).

He tends his flock like a shepherd:
He gathers the lambs in his arms
and carries them close to his heart;
he gently leads those that have young.
—Isaiah 40:11

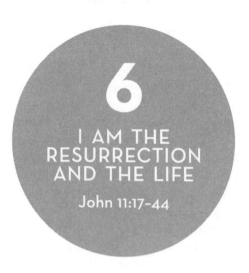

6

I AM THE RESURRECTION AND THE LIFE

John 11:17-44

Do not be afraid. I am the First and the Last. I am the Living One; I was dead, and now look, I am alive for ever and ever! And I hold the keys of death and Hades.
—Revelation 1:17b-18

From magnificent cathedrals in bustling cities to humble homes in remote mountains and deserts, the greeting is the same:

"He is risen!"

"He is risen, indeed!"

With that exchange of greetings comes the acknowledgment that life has triumphed over death! Forever! In the resurrection of Jesus from the dead, life wins!

The idea that life wins is an Easter certainty, but somehow we have tended to leave it to Easter to emphasize what should be the central affirmation of the Christian faith every day of the year. For many people, the test of that Easter greeting is greatest in the suffering and grief at the death of a loved one.

What does it really mean to say, "He is risen"? Is that more than an acknowledgment that Jesus has overcome the injustice and agony of his betrayal, cruel torture, and excruciating death on a Roman cross? Is it merely a seasonal greeting—one that holds no depth of truth to sustain us in the moments of searing loss when the worst possible news throws us to our knees?

The older we get, the more bad news we seem to get as the hardships of life take their toll on us and on those around us. My wife, Susan, and I have recently experienced loss as a result of both accident and disease. In each case the news was heartbreaking, the sense of loss and grief overwhelming. We have recently observed the stunning grief of a family whose college-age daughter was killed in an auto accident. The oppressive weight of grief and loss was obvious, the searing pain visible on the faces of the parents and siblings. We have also endured the grief of losing our parents, watching as the ravages of disease and age robbed our parents of their capabilities, their identities, and their lives. My own experience of losing a sibling to a sudden and devastating disease still causes moments of disbelief and pain.

Death is hard and harsh, even for those who believe in the promise of resurrection.

It's a stunning loss at the home in Bethany, near Jerusalem. There, two sisters find themselves immersed in despair when the lingering illness of their brother, Lazarus, ends in death. They have even reached out to their friend Jesus—the teacher, healer, and miracle worker—in a desperate plea for him to come to the bedside of Lazarus, the friend Jesus loves (see John 11:3).

Trust Is Assaulted by Loss (John 11:17-22)

As this passage unfolds before us, Jesus finally makes his way to Bethany. He has delayed his journey from the Jordan River valley to the home of his three close friends, even though the urgent message that came to him in Galilee left little doubt about the seriousness of the condition of Lazarus: "The one you love is sick" (v. 3).

In response to this plea for help, Jesus makes the puzzling decision to delay his departure for two days. The journey would take at least another full day, and in the interim before his arrival, Lazarus dies. Upon his arrival, he is told that Lazarus has been in the tomb for four days. It is lost on no one that, after four days, the processes of decay will have taken over. Death is so final!

Jesus's decision to delay his journey to Bethany confounds his dear friends and the concerned disciples. From the standpoint of the sisters, his timing is off—his arrival too late. From the standpoint of the disciples, his return to Judea is a recipe for disaster. The Jewish leaders have already been plotting his death, and it is certain that his being in proximity to Jerusalem will only give them greater opportunity to carry out their threats.

There is a tension in this narrative that is expressed by both the disciples and the sisters of Lazarus. If we misread this tension, we miss the point of this account.

When it becomes clear to his disciples that Jesus is going to Bethany (which is only two miles from Jerusalem), in spite of their protests and expressions of concern for his welfare, Thomas speaks with what could be read as a determined loyalty. Could it be that he simply refuses to give in to the fear that grips all the other disciples? "Let us also go, that we may die with him," says Thomas (v. 16). Does he grasp the severity of the threats against Jesus? Is he truly unwilling to abandon Jesus in this moment of danger?

On his arrival in Bethany, Martha speaks words of disappointment ("if you had been here . . ." [v. 21]), followed immediately by a deep expression of her faith in the relationship Jesus has with God: "But I know that even now God will give you whatever you ask" (v. 22). But this confident expression is still tinged with her sense of loss. She still believes that God the Father listens to Jesus, that Jesus has a very special relationship with God the Father—but there is no sense from Martha that this awful reality of death is anything but final.

The response of Thomas to Jesus's decision go to Bethany, over the objections of the disciples, reflects the sometimes grim determination shown by many to face the rigors of following Jesus, even to the point of death. Death is seen as a painful reality, forced upon us by circumstance or frailty, sometimes bearing with it the cynical assessment that life itself is a terminal disease. But is grim determination a kind of sacred fatalism? Are we left, in the final analysis, to a realization that *not even Jesus* can overcome the searing, painful reality that death and mortality are facts of our existence? Oh, there will be a resurrection—eventually, finally, at the last. But in the here and now, we must bow our heads into the turbulent winds of life and the inevitability of death, wrap our cloaks around us, and doggedly carry on until then.

Faith Is Awakened by Hope (John 11:23–37)

In response to both of Martha's statements, Jesus provides us with the central claim of the gospel of John and the major truth of the Christian faith. The theological center of this entire passage is contained in verses 25 and 26. Here we find the explanation for the miracle that occurs in verses 43 and 44, providing the meaning and significance of raising Lazarus from the dead in words that are timeless. While this miracle is noteworthy on many levels, the truths contained in verses 25 and 26 are the basis for our hope in the life of faith.

Ultimately, the faith that saves us is not our faith in the deeds and miracles of Jesus so much as our faith in the very *person* of Jesus. Our faith is not based on doctrine or particular events in the life of Jesus, or miracles he performed—as important and meaningful to us as these things are. That is the challenge Jesus presents over and over again to the Pharisees and the others gathered around him, pressing him for signs and miracles as a declaration of his identity and mission. But his words and his deeds are a continual effort to help everyone recognize who he is—which is why the "I am" sayings must have such meaning for us.

In every instance in which Jesus uses that poignant phrase, he is attempting to awaken the hearts and minds of the Jews to his true identity. He uses words that are embedded in their own heritage. The God they claim to know and follow identified himself to Moses as "I AM." Jesus's efforts to awaken them to his true mission can hardly be clearer than in

John 8:58. There, the Pharisees have been challenging his words with bitter criticism, refusing to believe his repeated insistence that he has been sent on this mission by "the Father." Every effort that Jesus can make to turn their hearts toward faith, he uses. In increasingly bold, challenging, and courageous statements, Jesus seeks to awaken the religious leaders and the people who have gathered around him to his true identity. But unbelief is stubbornly resistant to revelation, even when it is stunningly direct. When the Pharisees challenge his mastery over death, he answers them with words that are a clear, unequivocal claim to his true identity: "Before Abraham was born, I am!" (8:58).

It is not hidden from the people of Israel that Jesus is making bold claims. He is using their language. He is using their images and memories from their own prophetic writers. His words resonate with the people—especially the Pharisees—at profound levels. They just will not believe that what they have been looking forward to for so long could be coming to pass in this way, in this man, and at this time!

For all of these reasons, the story of the raising of Lazarus has great power. We who read these words in the twenty-first century have the hindsight of two thousand years of history and tradition. But for Martha and Mary, this is a moment of convulsive grief and confusion. They both express their sense of loss and confusion when they say, "If you had been here . . ." (11:21, 32). You can almost *still* hear the anguish in Martha's voice. She has come to trust Jesus at a deep level. She *knows* he could have healed her brother. But death is so final, even though there may be a hope that, eventually, Lazarus will live again.

But Jesus is not overwhelmed by this loss. He is not angry at their grief. He is not hesitant in the face of the Pharisees' doubt. And his words begin to awaken a new level of hope in Martha's grieving heart.

Death Is Defeated by Life (John 11:38–44)

Here is the moment of revelation that is the crux of all our hope. Here is the point toward which all the words of Jesus have been directed throughout his ministry. Here is the central reality on which our celebration of Easter stands to this very day: "Jesus said to her, 'I am the resurrection and the life. The one who believes in me will live, even though they die; and whoever lives by believing in me will never die'" (vv. 25–26a).

Jesus's promise does not mean that physical death is not real. And it does not mean that grief is not profoundly a part of human experience, even to this day. But it does mean that death is not *final*. It means that Jesus has accomplished a victory in his own resurrection that is the assurance that he has triumphed over death, sin, and hell. In his resurrection is our hope for our own resurrection, and for those who have placed their trust in him, death does not have the last word!

But there is more—much more! In the words of Jesus to Martha (vv. 23–25), we hear an assurance that is more central to the Christian faith than the promise of the eventual resurrection of the dead. The claim of the Christian faith is that in Christ—risen, ascended, and reigning as sovereign Lord—we may have a measure of life, a dimension of being, in this world, at this time, in this life, that is accessible through faith and based on the completed work of Jesus in his suffering death and resurrection.

When Jesus says to Martha, "I am the resurrection and the life," he is saying much more than that the dead will be raised. He is saying that the living may have life, available only through him—life as gift, life in depth, breadth, and dimension—unknown and unavailable until Jesus, the I AM, took on flesh and became human, assuming all the frailty and vulnerability of broken humanity.

This is the life made available to us when Jesus was raised from the dead on that first Easter morning. This is the life available to us as a gift of the Holy Spirit, poured out by the Father and the Son on the day of Pentecost. This is the life given in response to our faith in the promise of Jesus when he said, "I have come that they may have life, and have it to the full" (10:10). This is what we mean when we say that the kingdom of God has come and is now at work in our world. This is the already/not yet kingdom of God where we have life in him, and even though we die, we live.

We must not forget the way in which Jesus shares the grief of these heartbroken sisters. His own heart is deeply moved over the agony of suffering, of death, of disease, and of sin. When he makes his way to the tomb, hearing Mary express her own frustration and sorrow in those now familiar words, "If you had been here," Jesus grieves along with her. His grief is a powerful reminder of the fact that our own loss and suffering are not ignored or overlooked by God. Jesus, the I AM, is touched deeply by the grief of his friends. He weeps!

But his grief does not disrupt the objective Jesus has in this momentous event. He makes his way to the grave of Lazarus, accompanied by the sisters and their grieving friends. He intends to state once again, and in the clearest possible terms and actions, that he is indeed who he says he is. After a fervent and instructive prayer, Jesus raises his voice in command and shouts, "Lazarus, come out!" (11:43b).

To the astonishment of everyone, Lazarus does just that. At the mere command of Jesus, he comes out of the tomb! I AM has spoken!

The raising of Lazarus is another sign, a challenge to doubt, a fervent appeal to the hearts and minds of the people who have hung on his words, marveled at his miracles, and eaten bread and fish from his hands. Jesus offers so much more than bread, fish, sight for the blind, and healing from sickness or death. Death is vulnerable before Jesus not because of what Jesus can do. Death must release its grip on Lazarus because of who Jesus *is*.

Yet so many remain unconvinced.

On every Easter Sunday, when the Christian faith stops in wide-eyed wonder and marvels in remembrance of the stunning events of that day, it is important for us to once again be challenged by the words of Jesus to Martha: "I am the resurrection and the life. The one who believes in me will live, even though they die; and whoever lives by believing in me will never die. Do you believe this?" (vv. 25–26).

Do we believe it?

Therefore God exalted him to the highest place
and gave him the name that is above every name,
that at the name of Jesus every knee should bow,
in heaven and on earth and under the earth,
and every tongue acknowledge that Jesus Christ is Lord,
to the glory of God the Father.
—Philippians 2:9–11

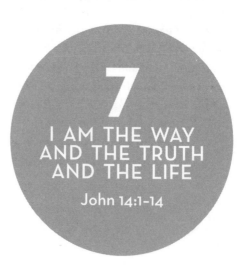

7

I AM THE WAY AND THE TRUTH AND THE LIFE

John 14:1-14

Whether you turn to the right or to the left, your ears will hear a voice behind you saying, "This is the way; walk in it."
—Isaiah 30:21

I once arrived for a meeting in a large, bustling, Asian city with no idea how to get to my intended destination. Previous arrangements had fallen apart after my departure from home, and it was now my responsibility to find my own way to the meeting. As I peered at the confusing maps and listened to the suggested routes offered by well-meaning guides, I was in a quandary. There seemed to be no clear guidance, and the distance to the site was considerable.

Then a man approached me, called my name, and introduced himself. To my delight and surprise, here was the host of the meeting, standing before me in the airport lobby. It was a great relief to hear him say, "I am here to take you to the meeting."

Maps, guides, and helpful instructions were not enough for me in that moment. I needed someone who could be "the way."

When Jesus came to earth, there were many who were willing to tell you how to get to God. The Pharisees insisted that the Law was the way.

You had to observe the regulations, offer the prescribed sacrifices, avoid working on the Sabbath, and keep away from the despised Gentiles. There were more rules and regulations than were possible to keep, but— since that was *the way*—you had no choice but to try.

Others said it was a futile effort. God was remote, the way to find him obscure, and the tragedies of life implied that he was, at best, indifferent to our concerns. After all, the promises had been many, but the reality was that Israel was weak, the Romans were in charge, and the prospects for change were slight. So why try at all?

But to the apostle John, there was hope, and his name was Jesus. Throughout the gospel that bears his name, the author presents an unfolding account of the life of this man Jesus. For John, there is no doubt about who Jesus is. And his gospel is written to make it as clear as possible that Jesus is unlike any man who has ever lived or will ever live again. Jesus is not just a remarkable teacher, a miracle worker, a politician, or an economist. This is the Son of God. This is the Creator of the universe stepping into human history as a baby, growing up as a man, and taking upon himself the mission of reconciling humanity to God.

In the developing story that John tells, he captures many of the images and memories of the people of Israel that have been written by prophets and historians throughout their history as a people. He reminds them of the promises God has made about why Israel is chosen, about what the mission for Israel has been and still is, and how Jesus is the fulfillment of all those hopes and dreams.

As he unfolds the story, John uses a variety of methods to make his point. Among them is the repeated expression of a term Jesus uses on several occasions. For John, each use is intended to convey in clear and unequivocal terms another development in the revelation as to who Jesus really is. Reaching into Israel's historic relationship to God, Jesus uses the term "I am" as a reference to one or another of the dimensions that describe himself and his mission.

Words of Comfort in the Face of Fear (John 14:1-4)

The scripture that is the focus of our attention in this chapter opens with a familiar passage that is often the centerpiece in memorial services for followers of Jesus. It is a source of abiding comfort in troubled times and deep assurance of our eternal hope. In the passage, Jesus speaks clearly to his disciples about his departure, his going away, his return to the Father. They are not aware of all that is implied in these statements, especially when Jesus says, "You know the way to the place where I am going" (v. 4). Jesus is preparing his disciples for what is about to occur within the next twenty-four hours. It is a perplexing time filled with uncertainty and foreboding. The tensions around them have been growing. The opponents of Jesus have become more vicious in their attacks. The future is filled with dire possibilities.

Jesus knows that the coming events will overwhelm his disciples. It is going to be a series of unbelievably traumatic experiences. The betrayal by Judas Iscariot will be a crushing and disorienting event. Who would imagine it? How could he do it? What was he thinking? What do you do when you are all blindsided by betrayal? As if that were not enough, the swirling and tumultuous events that will occur in the garden at Gethsemane, with the armed temple guards and the officials of the temple angrily seizing Jesus, will terrify the disciples. Their futile attempts at resistance will quickly end in their scattering in fear. Simon Peter, that most vocal of Jesus's followers, is quick to resist the suggestion that he might be so fickle as to ever deny Jesus. But what lies ahead for him will be the most crushing personal failure he has ever endured.

Jesus's words are carefully, deliberately, and personally directed toward those twelve men who have been with him for three years. They have heard his words, seen his miracles, eaten food he created out of almost nothing. They have experienced the wind-tossed sea growing suddenly and strangely calm at his word. They have come to believe that whatever he is going to do, they want to be a part of it all. But can they endure the stunning method by which he will accomplish his mission? Jesus knows that, determined as they are to follow him through whatever lies ahead, the disciples are simply not prepared for what he will endure. And it is for that very reason that his journey is so utterly necessary.

It is not surprising that these words have become so important to believers everywhere. They provide a source of incredible comfort when our world is shaking and the pieces of our lives are falling apart. But that comfort is possible only when these words are read in light of the events that unfolded over the course of the seventy-two hours after they were initially spoken. It is only because of what transpires in the life, death, and resurrection of Jesus that the words ring so genuinely true in our own hearts. The disciples are caught up in a maelstrom of betrayal, denial, torture, death, and burial. But it is *resurrection* that makes it possible for believers today to read the words of Jesus to the disciples with hope, even in the face of the most devastating realities.

Words of Guidance in the Midst of Confusion (John 14:5-7)

Thomas is that honest, candid disciple who always seems quickest to voice his concerns. He says to Jesus, "We don't know where you are going, so how can we know the way?" (v. 5). In response, Jesus utters what has become one of the most well-known and oft-quoted phrases in the New Testament: "I am the way and the truth and the life. No one comes to the Father except through me" (v. 6).

The Way

Unlike so many who oppose him, Jesus did not merely come to point the way to God and salvation. Jesus came to be the very embodiment *of* the way. His is not just a mission of information and direction. He came as the revelation of the Father, as the one who is not only able to give direction but also to provide the ability to know God, to enter into the kind of relationship with God that makes God present, real, accessible, and relevant. When Jesus says, "I am the way," he is not merely pointing in the right direction; he is taking them by the hand, strengthening them, guiding them, and accompanying them *along* the way.

Jesus is also revealing the character of God. Quite distinct from the vision of God presented by the Pharisees, Jesus refers to God with an endearing term that is unfamiliar to the Jews of that day. Repeatedly Jesus makes reference to "the Father." He insists that the Father is not distant, indifferent, or unapproachable. In fact, he claims that the Father sent him, that the Father dwells within him, and that he is going to the Father to prepare a place for them. When Jesus says, "I am the way," he is not just giving directions. He is inviting them into relationship with the Father who sent him.

The Truth

Throughout this gospel, John has been concerned with truth. He is especially concerned with truth as it relates to salvation—to knowing God. Repeatedly he makes reference to truth in this particular expression.

In telling the story, John frequently makes clear that, among many of those who are in positions of responsibility in Israel, there exists a gap between their teachings and their own lifestyles. They claim to be protectors of the truth while they live hollow and empty lives characterized by bitterness, hatred, and division. Even Herod Antipas, who claims the title "king of the Jews," is living in adultery. Many of the Pharisees—strict defenders of the Law—are confronted by Jesus for their devious efforts to keep the letter of the law while giving themselves permission to violate it in spirit, even as they impose harsh demands on others.

John is insistent that Jesus not only teaches with great insight and power but that he is the personification of the truth about which he teaches. It is one thing for a man to point to truth and affirm its value and worth. It is altogether another thing for a man to live in such a way that he becomes the model and example of the truth he so fervently teaches. Jesus can say with conviction and integrity, "I am the truth."

In Jesus, truth is not some high ideal, a set of principles to embrace, or a list of propositions to be memorized and believed. Truth is the holy

love of God embodied in passionate love for the Father, expressed con-
cretely in love for one another.

The Life

In the tenth chapter of John, where Jesus speaks of himself as the
gate for the sheep and as the good shepherd, we find one of those hope-
ful statements to which we cling with great tenacity. Jesus says, "I have
come that they [the sheep] may have life, and have it to the full" (10:10).
Here is where we may turn to grasp what Jesus means when he says, "I
am the life" in John 14:6.

Words of Revelation in Response
to Confusion (John 14:8–14)

Life is much more than a gift extended to us *by* Jesus. This is the
gift of the life *of* Jesus himself, imparted to his people through the Holy
Spirit. This is not an abstract idea of life as an ideal, as a zest for living,
or as an optimistic attitude toward things in life in spite of the baggage
we may carry. This is substantive. This is the being, the very self of
God, reaching to us, dwelling within us, embracing us, transforming us,
and enabling us.

While this is life with meaning and purpose, it is so much more than
that. This is life free from the tyranny of social acceptance or material
accumulation. This is life with hope. It is life filled with the anticipation
of what God has in store for us because, in Jesus, we have the very presence of the Father revealed to us. God is no longer removed, remote, or
shrouded in mystery. He has taken on a face, and it is the face of Jesus.

When the followers of Jesus—in light of his suffering death and
resurrection, his ascension to the right hand of the Father, and his presence given them in the Holy Spirit—grasp what Jesus has said in this
passage, it becomes a source of incredible promise. The works that Jesus
did, *we* can do—and even greater works. Sometimes we are confused or
disconcerted to believe that there is anything "greater" that we could do
than Jesus himself did. After all, the miracles of restored sight, of health

and physical wholeness, of broken and distributed food from only a boy's small lunch—these all seem so much greater than we could ever hope to do ourselves. We despair of our ability to do "greater" things.

But in ways that stagger the imagination, the followers of Jesus have altered the course of nations, have ministered help and hope in the face of devastation and disease, have established movements of compassion and selfless service that have touched people around the globe. Followers of Jesus—once few in number and limited to the tiny confines of Judea, Samaria, and Galilee—now number in the billions and are found in every nation of the world. They continue to spread and grow at levels only dimly conceived by those twelve men who heard him speak the words of hope and promise in an upper room in Jerusalem almost two thousand years ago. And the promises are unwavering. They still resonate, and the followers of Jesus still rely heavily on them. And if, in doing these greater things, we will call on the Spirit of Jesus for aid and strength to carry out this mission, he will provide everything we need.

This is life freely given us in Christ. Far from being the basis for claims of superiority over other religious persuasions, this is a celebration that God has reached to a fallen and broken world in Christ. Through us he has offered the world and everyone in it the opportunity to experience God, to see him with the eyes of faith, and to know him even as we are known by him. This is our grand hope because Jesus is our access to the Father! And he is the access—the unique and sufficient way—to God for every man, woman, and child on the face of the earth. Jesus, is the Way, the Truth, and the Life!

This is our holy hope, and this is our global mission!

Commit your way to the Lord;
trust in him and he will do this:
He will make your righteous reward shine like the dawn,
your vindication like the noonday sun.
—Psalm 37:5-6

8

I AM THE
TRUE VINE

John 15:1-17

As the rain and the snow
come down from heaven,
and do not return to it
without watering the earth
and making it bud and flourish,
so that it yields seed for the sower and bread for the eater,
so is my word that goes out from my mouth:
It will not return to me empty,
but will accomplish what I desire
and achieve the purpose for which I sent it.
—Isaiah 55:10-11

They are scattered across much of the Middle East, often in places you would not expect. But the vineyards of Israel are remarkable. Some of them stretch for hundreds of yards across barren landscape that would seem altogether inhospitable to a growing crop of delicious grapes. The practice of viticulture—the cultivation of grapevines for the purpose of producing fruit, juice, and wine—is a vital part of the Israeli economy. Their wines are sold around the world. Wine has been vital to that part of the world and other parts of the world as well, as an alternative source of hydration to the often-polluted water. Prior to the development of water-purification methods, wine was safer to drink than water from standing pools or cisterns.

Vineyards are not at all new to this part of the world, so the image of the vine and its branches is instantly recognizable to the disciples of Jesus. This is a familiar image not only because of the readily apparent vineyards found in and around the villages and towns of Israel but also because of the frequent use of the image of the vine in the religious heritage of Israel.

There are many references to Israel itself as a vineyard in the prophetic writings and in the Psalms. The prophet Isaiah likened Israel to a vineyard, saying, "The vineyard of the LORD Almighty is the nation of Israel, and the people of Judah are the vines he delighted in" (5:7a). But the image of Israel as a vine was often a negative reference. In "The Song of the Vineyard" in Isaiah 5, the prophet spoke of God's despair at finding that the vineyard yielded only bad grapes when God expected to find good.

Jesus often turns to the book of Isaiah to dig into the memories and capture the attention of his listeners. He reads from the scroll of the prophet Isaiah in Nazareth when he begins his ministry. Three years later, as he spends time on that final evening with his disciples in the Passover celebration, he once again turns to an image found in Isaiah.

However, in applying the image of the vine, Jesus makes a significant change. Where Isaiah connected the vine to the people of Israel, Jesus attaches *himself* to the image, completely redefining the symbol of the vine. "I am the true vine," he says, "and my Father is the gardener" (John 15:1). In this, he does not simply adapt the image of the vine to suggest that he is now the true Israel. It might be tempting to believe that, when he shifts the image of the vine from Israel to himself, Jesus is indicating the rejection of Israel. But there is a greater purpose in the life and ministry of Jesus. Jesus does indeed fulfill the mission that was originally given to the children of Abraham, but it is essential to remember the words of the apostle Paul in his letter to the Romans. The mission of Jesus does *not* imply a rejection of Israel as God's covenant people. Rather, the mission of Jesus brings to fulfillment the plan of redemption for all humanity. Paul makes it clear in Romans that *all have sinned:* "There is no one righteous, not even one; there is no one who understands; there is no one who seeks God. All have turned away, they have together become worthless; there is no one who does good, not even one" (3:10–12).

For Jesus, as for Paul, the importance that Jesus be understood as the true vine does not so much mean the rejection of Israel as it does the inclusion of the Gentiles. The mission of Jesus is to accomplish the redemption of all humanity. Jesus is not abandoning the people of Israel. Rather, he is describing the nature of the relationship between himself and God, and with the community of his followers. This is a radically relational image, describing the depth of relationship between the Father and Jesus and between Jesus and his followers. The objective of the relationship he describes is that the branches might bear fruit, and all three figures—the gardener, the vine, and the branches—are essential to the production of good fruit and the fulfillment of the mission.

Throughout this segment of the gospel, the writer makes great theological use of the metaphor of the vine and the branches. This is not just for the purpose of accessing a familiar image to make a point. John allows the metaphor to bear a load of insight and understanding into the very nature of the relationship between the Father, the Son, and the believing community. The image becomes more an allegory than a metaphor since the details of the metaphor bear so much weight throughout this passage. Jesus is preparing his disciples for what lies ahead of them in the long term. This is the preparation of the disciples for the ongoing life of the church.

The Work of the Gardener (John 15:1–4)

Few images are more important for us than the image of God the Father as the Gardener. Jesus is returning to the previous section of this discourse. In 14:28, he says, "If you loved me, you would be glad that I am going to the Father, for the Father is greater than I." As he has done repeatedly in the gospel of John, Jesus reminds his disciples that everything he does is done at the direction of the Father.

Dr. Dennis Kinlaw once said that it was years before he realized that the central figure in the gospel of John is not Jesus but, rather, "the Father who sent me." Repeatedly Jesus speaks of his utter and complete dependence on the Father. The work he does, the words he speaks, the purpose for which he has come are all at the instigation and for the sake of the Father. Jesus makes that very point for his disciples when he says to them, "My Father is the gardener" (15:1).

The work of the gardener is to care for the vineyard—to cultivate it, water it, and protect it from invasive pests and marauding thieves. This is demanding work that requires a consuming measure of personal investment in the welfare of the vineyard. The gardener at times appears ruthless in evaluating the health of the vine. Unfruitful branches are removed, cut off. Fruit-bearing branches are trimmed back, pruned, cleaned of excess foliage that would drain away the nutrients necessary for the production of fruit. Everything that hinders the production of fruit is done away with.

It would be easy to be distracted by this passage, wondering about the process of cutting off the branches that do not bear fruit and the pruning back of those branches that do bear fruit. It could become a fruitless and dangerous pursuit to attribute motives to God in the events and traumas that we encounter in our personal lives. For the faithful follower of Christ, the point of the passage is the intensely direct involvement of the Gardner and the security and safety of abiding in the Vine. That the follower of Christ is not exempt from suffering and loss is an obvious reality, but it is the point of this passage that fruit-bearing is the natural result of abiding and that our ability to abide in the Vine is a gift of grace from the hand of the Gardener, who shapes and cares for the branches that are healthily embedded in the Vine.

The Role of the Vine (John 15:5–8)

Throughout the final evening with his disciples, Jesus makes clear his desires for his frightened and uncertain followers. They face an unknown and disturbing future. He assures them of his intense and sacrificial love for them. His relationship with them is the means by which they have access to the Father. God is the source and guiding hand that directs the work of Jesus. Jesus is the true vine because he came from the Father, just as he is the true light and the true bread from heaven.

It is the intent of Jesus throughout the "I am" sayings in this gospel to declare his utter dependence on and obedience to the Father. His role is not in isolation as a heroically sacrificial leader seeking to establish a new religious movement in Israel. He has come as the embodiment of the very being of God. But Jesus, as the Vine, is utterly committed to the Gardner. The care, the purposes, and the means by which those purposes are to be fulfilled all lie in the hands of the Gardner. Jesus's obedience to the Father and his constant references to his dependence on the Father make the figure of the Gardner essential to our understanding of the importance of this passage of Scripture. As clearly as anywhere else in Scripture, Jesus declares that it is "the Father who sent me" who has initiated, sustained, and fulfilled the mission of the redemption of all humanity: "For God so loved the world . . ." (3:16).

But in the image of the vineyard, Jesus also stresses the interdependence of the branches and the vine. The people of Israel are being invited into a new and transforming relationship with the God who formed them, drew them into relationship with himself, and gave them the mission to be light to the Gentiles. For the most part, the Jews are so blinded by their own expectations and agendas that they cannot see Jesus for who he really is. But to his followers, Jesus gives this gracious assurance: "I am the vine; you are the branches" (15:5a). Branches are not capable of surviving on their own. Their very lives are dependent on the sustenance and nutrition provided by the vine. That vine is everything to the branches, just as the gardener is the necessary and vital resource for the vine.

The Responsibility of the Branches (John 15:9–17)

Just as the vine is dependent on the care and attention of the gardener, so the branches are utterly dependent on the vine for their very existence. Just as the vine is not self-sufficient, so the branches are not self-originating.

Throughout my adult life, I have been fascinated by viticulture. Although by conviction and practice I totally abstain from all alcoholic beverages, I find the discipline and science of growing grapevines for fruit and beverage an engaging subject. In my visits to various parts of the world, I have seen vineyards in a variety of settings. Though some grapevines are intertwined over a trellis at the entrance to a yard and some are used as shade on a pergola, most vineyards are anything but decorative. The purpose of a vineyard is to produce fruit. The appearance of the vine is not the issue. In fact, the most productive vineyards often seem to be scrawny, sparse, and visually unattractive. But I have never met a gardener who did not think their vineyard was attractive. There is a deep love for the care of the vines, and almost constant attention is given to seeing that the vine and branches are properly cared for in order to achieve maximum productivity.

There is no secondary value to the discarded branches of a grapevine. They are not useful for any productive purpose, including fire. The wood burns quickly and produces little lasting heat. Aside from being united to the vine, fruit-bearing is everything!

Jesus also makes it very clear that the ability of the branches to bear fruit is wholly dependent on their remaining connected to the vine. Just as the vine is the necessary source for sustenance and nutrition for the branches, so the branches are responsible to abide—to remain connected to the vine. Jesus applies this image to the relationship he has with his disciples. Their ability to remain in Jesus is dependent on his remaining in them (15:4). This is the work of grace—a recognition that, while there is a responsibility on the part of the vine, even the capability of exercising that responsibility is a result of the grace of the Gardener.

In verses 5 and 6, and even further in verses 9–17, the image shifts focus from the actions of God as gardener and Jesus as the vine to the responsibilities of the branches themselves. Here the agricultural imagery is folded into theological language. Jesus speaks with clarity and directness when he says to the disciples, "If you remain in me and I in you, you will bear much fruit" (v. 5b). But note especially the clear warning to the disciples: "If you do not remain in me, you are like a branch that is thrown away and withers" (v. 6a). The emphasis here is not on the production of fruit. It is on the necessity of a relationship with Jesus. Fruit is the natural product of a healthy relationship. It may be that pruning and cleaning are necessary, but such pruning and cleaning are a far distance away from what it means to be separated from the vine and thrown away.

Jesus's words must not be lost on us. To remain in Jesus, and for him to remain in us, is the essential condition of fruit-bearing. The striving and straining that are often associated with being fruitful miss the point. The essential need is to remain in relationship with God and to cultivate that relationship above all other things. In response to a healthy and growing relationship of trusting obedience to God, fruit is produced, love reigns, and communion between God and God's people is assured.

And what is the fruit that we will bear? It is to remain in his love. It is to obey his commands. And what is his command? "Love each other as I have loved you" (v. 12b). It is to lay down our lives for our brothers and sisters, both those near to us and those far away. It is to reflect in tangible ways in the community of faith what it meant for Jesus to kneel at the dirty feet of his disciples and wash them. It is to bear toward a broken and alienated world with the redeeming love of God. It is to bask in the love of God for us and to pour that love out on others.

Then, with faith strong and love for others burning in our souls, we will know how to pray for those things that delight the heart of God, and we will find the words of Jesus to be true: "Ask whatever you wish, and it will be done for you" (v. 7b).

The land yields its harvest;
God, our God, blesses us.
May God bless us still,
so that all the ends of the earth will fear him.
—Psalm 67:6–7

AFTERWORD:
THE MISSING "I AM"

As I have pondered the importance of the seven "I am" sayings of Jesus in the gospel of John, I have been struck by the breadth of their descriptive power. The writer of the gospel of John is strategic in the use of Jesus's words. Throughout the gospel, the writer focuses the attention of the reader on the developing realization that this man—this miracle worker, this teacher—is far more than those who hear him in person initially can comprehend.

The "I am" sayings are intended to reveal something beyond what even the prophets imagined. Jesus, in this gospel, reveals himself to his disciples and to those who are willing and able to hear him as more than a rabbi, more than a miracle worker, more than a prophet. For his disciples, his references to the Father are unlike any language they have heard before. His intimacy with "the Father who sent me," his insistence that he does nothing apart from the Father, his frequent getaways to spend time in conversation with the Father, are intended to be signposts that will grab their attention and turn their hearts and minds toward his true identity.

The seven sayings we have examined are accessed by the writer of the gospel of John as descriptors of the multifaceted ministry of Jesus, gathered from the events in his life and attached to the life and experience of the people with whom he walks and talks. They express the broad range of his work. His use of metaphor and parable, his engagement in the textures of the culture, and his deliberate attempts to give definition to his identity and his mission make the sayings a critical resource for understanding who Jesus is and what he came to do.

For that reason, I was struck by the idea that there seemed to be a missing "I am." Since the sayings are all drawn from common and understandable images and symbols, how is it that there is so much reference to water in the gospel, yet there is no account of Jesus utilizing that metaphor directly in an "I am" saying? Jesus's miracle at the wedding in Cana of Galilee is the first of many mentions of water in and around the activities of Jesus. There is his baptism and his offer of living water to the Samaritan woman at the well. There is the healing at the Pool of Siloam and his walking on the water.

At the Festival of Tabernacles in John 7:37–39, we have the most direct and revealing use of the metaphor of water as a direct reference to the work of Jesus. At the Festival of Tabernacles, the priest poured water drawn from one of the wells in Jerusalem. The altar in the temple was circled with the freshly drawn water, poured out as a libation to God. It was a high moment in each day of the festival and was often accompanied by praises lifted toward heaven. In John 7, they are halfway through the festival, and Jesus has gone up to the temple and begun to teach the people gathered there. Many have anticipated his coming, and the tension only increases as those who oppose him and those who follow him respond to his teaching. On the last day of the festival, perhaps after the final libation has been poured out around the altar, Jesus stands and cries out, "Let anyone who is thirsty come to me and drink. Whoever believes in me, as Scripture has said, rivers of living water will flow from within them" (vv. 37b–38).

I would expect this to be an ideal moment for Jesus to make another claim to his identity. "I am the water of life," he might say. After all, his being the source of living water is, by this time in the gospel, well established. He has already said to the Samaritan woman, "If you knew the gift of God and who it is that asks you for a drink, you would have asked him and he would have given you living water" (4:10). Later he says to her, "Everyone who drinks this water will be thirsty again, but whoever drinks the water I give them will never thirst. Indeed, the water I give them will become in them a spring of water welling up to eternal life" (vv. 13–14). So why doesn't Jesus just say it? Why not give us one more of those gripping expressions that resonate across the centuries?

There is a stunning turn in the conversation with the woman, which the gospel writer seems to highlight intentionally. The expectations of the Samaritan woman are expressed in eschatological terms. A Messiah is to come, and he will explain everything. But in this encounter, Jesus turns the expectation of a future, eschatological new age on its head. *Certainly a time is coming,* he says. But then he brings a completely new dimension into the conversation. The time "has now come" (v. 23)! The issue is no longer where the people are to worship—whether in Samaria or in Jerusalem. The reality is no longer geographical. It is personal! Those who worship God are to worship in the Spirit and in truth. The Messiah who is to come *has* come. The one speaking to you is the I AM (v. 26)!

While the NIV and the NRSV both translate the phrase on the lips of Jesus as, "I am he," the Greek is much more definitive. It confirms the purpose for which the other seven "I am" sayings are conveyed. In this case, the statement is far more than a mere identification of Jesus as the one who is to come. This is considered by scholars as one of the absolute uses of "I am." There is no predicate nominative ("I am the bread of life"). This is an unequivocal reach back into Israel's ancient past when God identified himself to Moses as "I AM" (Exodus 3:14–16).

Here Jesus offers to the Samaritan woman one of the most definitive revelations of his person that can be found in the gospel of John. Even his disciples have not yet heard it in quite this way. They will later, when tossed about by a violent storm on the Lake of Galilee. Already terrified by the storm, they are stunned to see someone walking toward them on the water. His words to them, not readily seen in our English translations, are, "I AM. Do not be afraid" (John 6:20).

We must carefully handle all this material, especially as it relates to our study of the "I am" sayings of Jesus. We cannot read more into the material than is warranted by later scholarship and the work of the ecumenical councils in the early church. But perhaps the early councils were informed as much by the gospel of John as by the writings of Paul.

While there is no definitive description of a Trinitarian concept of the Godhead in the gospel, it is altogether possible that the clues left by the writer—giving as true an account of the nature and work of Jesus the Messiah as could be given—create the foundation upon which the idea could be formed. Throughout the gospel of John are clear references to a relationship between Jesus and "the Father." While there are clearly distinctive aspects to each of the persons, the essential unity is often expressed (see John 1:1; 17:1–12).

In the account of Jesus at the Festival of Tabernacles, Jesus cries out "in a loud voice," inviting all who hear to "come to me and drink" (7:37). But the writer makes a clear and definitive statement that Jesus is making reference to "the Spirit" (v. 39). There are repeated references to "the Spirit" in the gospel of John (see especially chapters 14, 15, and 16). And there is the final reference to the resurrected Jesus breathing on the disciples and saying to them, "Receive the Holy Spirit" (20:22).

It is interesting how often the concept of the Spirit is related to references to water in the gospel of John. Perhaps we should see in these many references to the Spirit on the lips of Jesus an objective reference to the Spirit in ways that make it unlikely he will, or can, voice an "I am" statement that references himself. Could it be that he is protecting that expression for the one to whom it more properly belongs—the Spirit?

While we must understand that the conception of God as triune was articulated only over a period of centuries, it is obvious in retrospect that the writer of the gospel is conveying to us a grasp of the foundations on which a Trinitarian concept of God can be formed. We must not read back into the gospel an intent that is not present in the mind of the writer or in the conception of the early church, but we may indeed celebrate that our ability to see Trinitarian implications is not contrived or inaccurately read into the text.

For that reason, I come to rest. Jesus promises with conviction that the Spirit is a source of life and strength, of instruction and counsel, of advocacy and purity. The Spirit will carry on into the future the work, the life, the redemption, and the promises of Jesus. The Spirit is the spring of living water, pouring out of the believer and into the world as we know it, making present, contemporary, and effectual the life, death, and resurrection of Jesus.

Thanks be to God!